Merry Christmas!

Inspiring Quotes, Poems, and Stories to Celebrate the Season

Honor Books
Tulsa, Oklahoma

Merry Christmas
Inspiring Quotes, Poems, and Stories to Celebrate the Season
ISBN 1-56292-635-7
Copyright © 1999 by Honor Books
P.O. Box 55388
Tulsa, Oklahoma 74155

Creative ideas to help celebrate the season written by Dianna Platner, Ph.D.

Introduction

Christmas is in the air again. Is there anything more wonderful than this season of love, peace, and goodwill? People smile more. Carols ring through every store. Bustling shoppers comb the aisles looking for just the right gift. Mulled cider scents the air, and we cuddle in front of crackling fireplaces, snug and warm despite a windy chill.
Merry Christmas! Joyeux Noël! Feliz Navidad! Buon Natale!

Merry Christmas *is designed to capture all the sights, sounds, scents, and sentiments of this glorious holiday. The reason for the season can be so powerful that it's hard to express the story we'd like to share with family and friends.* ***Merry Christmas*** *offers just the right words to bring holiday cheer to the ones who deserve much more than a card and to celebrate the birth of the Christ Child.*

Honor Books offers suggestions to make the holiday a more meaningful experience for people of all ages. Make ***Merry Christmas*** *a daily part of your own Christmas season.*

GREETINGS FROM AROUND THE WORLD

Italian: Buon Natale! (Good Christmas)

Swedish: God Jul! (Good Yule)

French: Joyeux Noël! (Joyous Christmas)

Danish: Glædelig Jul! (Glad Yule)

Portuguese: Bonas Festas! (Good Holidays)

7

I've seen the face of Jesus . . . It was a wondrous sight!

Oh, glorious face of beauty, oh gentle touch of care;

If here it is so blessed, what will it be up there?

W. SPENCER WALTON

THE WORD BECAME FLESH AND MADE HIS
DWELLING AMONG US. WE HAVE SEEN HIS
GLORY, THE GLORY OF THE ONE AND ONLY,
WHO CAME FROM THE FATHER, FULL OF
GRACE AND TRUTH.

JOHN 1:14

If you hitch your wagon to a star, be sure it's

the Star of Bethlehem.

THE MORNING STARS SANG TOGETHER AND
ALL THE ANGELS SHOUTED FOR JOY.

JOB 38:7

SPECIAL THINGS TO DO ON THE DAYS
LEADING UP TO CHRISTMAS

- *Wake everyone up with a hearty, "Merry Christmas!"*

- *Turn on the Christmas tree lights while getting ready for school and work.*

- *Serve breakfast on Christmas china.*

- *Pack a candy cane or a piece of holiday chocolate in your family's lunches.*

- *Play Christmas music to start the day with cheer.*

CHRISTMAS IN RUSSIA

Even though Christmas was first introduced into Russia more than a thousand years ago when Great Duke Vladimir of the Russian Royal family converted to Christianity, it was not until the early eighteenth century that the celebration was Westernized. Czar Peter the Great introduced a great many Western European practices, including the traditional evergreen Christmas tree, that was decorated with apples, candy, nuts, and candles.

*After the Bolshevik Revolution in 1917,
Christmas trees and all religious celebrations and
symbols were banned under the atheistic government.
The holiday commemorating the birth of Christ was
changed to the Festival of Winter. Beautiful blown-
glass, or Dresden-type ornaments decorated the
evergreen, renamed the New Year's Tree.*

*In 1991, after the fall of Communism in
Russia, the people were able to celebrate their first
real Christmas in seventy-five years.*

Merry Christmas

FOR TO US A CHILD IS BORN, TO US A SON IS
GIVEN, AND THE GOVERNMENT WILL BE ON HIS
SHOULDERS. AND HE WILL BE CALLED
WONDERFUL COUNSELOR, MIGHTY GOD,
EVERLASTING FATHER, PRINCE OF PEACE.

ISAIAH 9:6

JESUS

Wonderful—He would be wonderful in what He would accomplish for the fallen human race.

Counselor—He would be our Guide through life, and our Advocate before the Heavenly Father.

The Mighty God—He would be the God before Whom every knee shall one day bow.

The Everlasting Father—He would be the God of eternity.

The Prince of Peace—He would be the One Who would ultimately bring a true tranquillity among all nations.

KENNETH W. OSBECK

WHAT CHILD IS THIS?

What Child is this, Who, laid to rest,
on Mary's lap is sleeping?
Whom angels greet with anthems sweet,
while shepherds watch are keeping?
This, this is Christ, the King,
Whom shepherds guard and angels sing;
Haste, haste to bring Him laud,
the Babe, the Son of Mary.

SHE GAVE BIRTH TO HER FIRSTBORN, A SON.
SHE WRAPPED HIM IN CLOTHS AND PLACED
HIM IN A MANGER, BECAUSE THERE WAS NO
ROOM FOR THEM IN THE INN.

LUKE 2:7

The best Christmas gift of all

is the presence of a happy family

all wrapped up with one another.

CHRISTMAS IN THE UNITED STATES

- *In Washington, D.C., a huge, spectacular tree (considered the National Christmas Tree) is lit ceremoniously by the President.*

- *In Boston, carol singing festivities are famous. The singers are accompanied by hand bells.*

- *In the state of Missouri, roast turkey or ham, mashed potatoes and gravy, green bean casserole, and cranberry sauce are Christmas meal favorites.*

- *In Hawaii, Christmas starts with the coming of the Christmas Tree Ship, bringing a great load of Christmas fare. Santa Claus also arrives by boat.*

- *In California, Santa Claus sweeps in on a surfboard.*

THE FIRST NATIONAL CHRISTMAS TREE

The American tradition of lighting a National Christmas Tree was instituted in 1923 by President Calvin Coolidge. On Christmas Eve of that year, the President walked to the darkened tree and pressed a switch with his foot to turn on the 3,000 bulbs.

Unlike more modern Presidents, Coolidge gave no Christmas address, even though the event, featuring Christmas carols and the Marine Band, was broadcast by radio to more than a million people!

In 1927, President Coolidge sent Christmas greetings to the nation, written on White House stationery in his own hand. It was printed in American newspapers on Christmas Day.

∽

Christmas is not a time or a season but a state of mind. To cherish peace and good will, to be plenteous in mercy, is to have the real spirit of Christmas. If we think on these things there will be born in us a Savior and over us all will shine a star, sending its gleam of hope to the world.

CALVIN COOLIDGE

DID YOU KNOW?

In 1804, American soldiers at Fort Dearborn, Illinois, decorated one of the first American Christmas trees.

CHRISTMAS IN THE UNITED KINGDOM

Children write their requests in letters to Father Christmas, but instead of dropping them into the mailbox, they toss them into the fireplace. According to legend, the draft carries the letters up the chimney, and Father Christmas reads the smoke.

When the younger children wake early on Christmas morning, they find stockings at the ends of their beds and a few presents on the floor. Later, the whole family gathers around the lighted tree to open the rest of the presents.

HOME-MADE EGGNOG

12 large eggs
1 can evaporated skim milk, 13 oz.
1 cup confectioner's sugar
Nutmeg

*Beat the eggs together in a large bowl until foamy.
Add milk and sugar. Stir. Strain mixture through
sieve and pour into jar. Close lid and chill. Sprinkle
nutmeg on top when ready to serve.*

BIRD OF DAWNING

Some say that ever 'gainst that season comes
Wherein our Saviour's birth is celebrated,
The bird of dawning singeth all night long:
And then, they say, no spirit dare stir abroad;
The nights are wholesome; then no planets strike,
No fairy takes, nor witch hath power to charm,
So hallow'd and so gracious is the time.

WILLIAM SHAKESPEARE

Heap on more wood!
The wind is chill;
But let it whistle
As it will.
We'll keep
Our Christmas
Merry still.

SIR WALTER SCOTT

DECORATING WITH CANDLES
AND EVERGREENS

The flicker of white candlelight and the scent of fresh evergreens and apples combine to create an appealing, inexpensive, and easy-to-arrange centerpiece for a holiday table.

Fill hollowed-out red or green apples with votive candles or tea lights, and insert into a floral-foam base with floral picks. Arrange fresh-cut evergreens around the apples. Accent with little red birds and bright red-and-green plaid ribbon.

CHRISTMAS TIME

Christmas time is here once again
Snow is falling softly again
It's the time of year
When everyone belongs together
Never mind the cold or the weather
Take a chance
Share some love
Christmas time is here once again
People stop to talk with a friend
Say a kindly word
And everything seems so much better
Little things, they don't seem to matter
Take a chance
Share some love

GRACE LUCAS

CHRISTMAS DURING
THE GREAT DEPRESSION

President Herbert Hoover's administration (1929 to 1932) was plagued by the devastating drought that brought on the Great Depression. With much of the country out of work, Christmas celebrations were lean, and many children found no presents at all under the tree. The church grew stronger, and people were helpful to one another.

During the Hoovers' first Christmas Eve dinner party, a fire broke out in the West Wing, destroying the President's desk. The Marine Band loudly played Christmas carols to drown out the sound of fire engines. Later, souvenirs were carved from the desk for White House staffers, making the best of a difficult situation.

FUN GIFT EXCHANGES

- *White elephants. Something used, but useful.*

- *Favorite book. Write in the front what it has meant to you.*

- *Cookies. Bring 1/2 dozen of your favorite Christmas cookies and the recipe on a 3 x 5 card for each person attending.*

- *Ornaments. Unique and under $10.00 each.*

- *Picture frames. Unique and under $10.00 each.*

In 1948, President Harry S. Truman gave all his staffers a brown leather bookmark for Christmas. It was embossed with his personal motto:

I would rather have peace in the world than be President.

KIDS' COOKING GUIDELINES

- *Wash your hands with soap and hot water.*

- *Put on an apron to protect your clothing.*

- *Open the cookbook to the page with your recipe.*

- *Gather and measure all the ingredients needed to prepare your dish.*

- *Always call a parent if your recipe calls for the use of the oven, stove, or microwave.*

- *Have fun!*

CHRISTMAS CANDLE DESSERT
JUST FOR KIDS!

Ingredients:
4 sugar cookies
4 slices of canned pineapple
2 bananas
4 teaspoons of whipped cream
4 maraschino cherries

Place one sugar cookie on each plate.
Lay a pineapple slice on top of each cookie.
Stand ½ banana in the hole of each pineapple.
Top each banana with a bit of whipped cream and a cherry.
(Serves 4)

Jesus is the reason for the season!

CHRISTMAS IN INDIA

Although Christians are a minority in India, Christmas is still a festive celebration. Decorated mango and banana trees replace the more traditional evergreens. Some houses use mango leaves inside the house, and others line their flat roofs and walls with small clay oil-burning lamps. For the Christmas Eve service, churches are decorated with poinsettias and brightly lit candles.

"Silent Night" was written in 1818 by an Austrian priest named Joseph Mohr. He was told the day before Christmas that the church organ was broken and would not be repaired in time for Christmas Eve. He was saddened by this and could not imagine Christmas without music. Deciding to compose a carol that could be sung by the choir to guitar music, he sat down and immediately wrote three stanzas. Later that night, the people in the little Austrian Church sang "Stille Nacht" for the first time.

Let's allow the joy of Christ's birth

to be reflected on our faces and heard in our glad

singing of praises to Him all through this

Christmas season.

SILENT NIGHT, HOLY NIGHT

Silent night! Holy night! All is calm, all is bright,
Round yon virgin mother and Child,
Holy Infant, so tender and mild,
Sleep in heavenly peace, sleep in heavenly peace.

Silent night! Holy night! Shepherds quake at the sight;
Glories stream from heaven afar;
Heav'nly hosts sing alleluia
Christ the Savior is born! Christ the Savior is born!

Silent Night! Holy Night! Son of God, love's pure light
Radiant beams from Thy holy face
With the dawn of redeeming grace
Jesus, Lord at Thy birth, Jesus, Lord at Thy birth.

Silent Night, Holy night! All is calm, all is bright
Sleep in heavenly peace.

JOSEPH MOHR

CREATIVE CHRISTMAS WRAPPING
FOR CHILDREN

White lunch bags
Holiday cookie cutters
Pencil

Crayons
Single-hole punch
Flat ribbon

On the white bag, trace the shape of the cookie cutter with a pencil. Use the crayons to color and decorate the designs. Place the gift inside. Fold over one to two inches at the top of the bag and punch two holes about an inch apart. Run ribbon through the holes, and tie a bow on the front of the package. Bag may be personalized with crayons.

THE PERFECT GIFTS FOR GRANDPARENTS

- *A picture of yourself*

- *A homemade card*

- *A letter written from your heart*

- *A big hug and kiss*

- *The gift of time*

- *A live plant*

- *A box of peppermint sticks*

Laughter is the sweetest music

that ever greeted the human ear.

OUR MOUTHS WERE FILLED WITH LAUGHTER,
OUR TONGUES WITH SONGS OF JOY. THEN IT WAS
SAID AMONG THE NATIONS, "THE LORD HAS
DONE GREAT THINGS FOR THEM."

PSALM 126:2

CREATIVE WAYS TO PERSONALIZE
YOUR CHRISTMAS CARDS

- *Tape a family picture inside.*

- *Enclose a favorite family recipe on a 3 x 5 card, with the name of the relative you associate with it.*

- *Enclose a one-page Holiday Update to share what's going on in your family.*

- *Copy and enclose a cherished family holiday poem.*

- *Inside the cover, pen your favorite Scripture focusing on Jesus.*

CHRISTMAS IN NORWAY

The Nordic tradition of burning a yule log dates back to medieval times. Originally, an entire tree was carefully chosen and brought into the house with great ceremony. The large end of the tree would be placed into the fireplace, while the rest of it stuck out into the room. The yule log would be lit from the remains of the previous year's log, which had been stored away for the occasion, and it would be fed slowly into the fire through the twelve days of Christmas.

From a little spark may burst a mighty flame.

DANTE

THEREFORE THE LORD HIMSELF WILL GIVE
YOU A SIGN: THE VIRGIN WILL BE WITH
CHILD AND WILL GIVE BIRTH TO A SON, AND
WILL CALL HIM IMMANUEL.

ISAIAH 7:14

Tell me the story of Jesus,
Write on my heart every word;

Tell me the story most precious,
Sweetest that ever was heard.

Tell how the angels, in chorus,
Sang as they welcomed His birth,

"Glory to God in the highest!
Peace and good tiding to earth."

FANNY J. CROSBY

Be so in tune with the exultant song of the angels

during this Christmas season that others may see

and hear that Christ dwells with you.

AN ANGEL OF THE LORD APPEARED TO THEM,
AND THE GLORY OF THE LORD SHONE AROUND
THEM, AND THEY WERE TERRIFIED.

LUKE 2:9

GIVE FROM THE HEART

After the Thanksgiving turkey is gobbled up, place a cup in the center of your kitchen table. Each time you sit down for dinner, empty your pocket change into it. A few days before Christmas, contribute the funds to the church mission collection, a charitable organization, or a nearby shelter for abused mothers. You'll be surprised how fast the money adds up, and your children will learn a valuable lesson about sharing.

NANCY B. GIBBS

The only blind person at Christmastime is he

who has not Christmas in his heart.

HELEN KELLER

It is Christmas in the mansion,
  Yule-log fires and silken frocks,

It is Christmas in the cottage,
  Mother's filling little socks.

It is Christmas on the highway,
  In the thronging, busy mart.

But the dearest, truest Christmas
  Is the Christmas in the heart.

SENTIMENTAL GIFTS FOR LOVED ONES

- *Ornaments home-made out of old lace tablecloths.*

- *A favorite family recipe passed down through the generations.*

- *A piece of art made of the children's handprints and fingerpaint.*

- *Cuttings from your favorite greenhouse plants, potted in a small vase that is wrapped in a holiday bow.*

Two marks of a Christian:

giving and forgiving.

YUMMY IDEAS FOR THE
CHRISTMAS SEASON

- *Leave goodies in your mailbox for your mail carrier.*

- *Invite a few women for a cookie exchange party. Ask each one to bake a dozen cookies to enjoy and share and an extra dozen to give away.*

- *Plan a progressive dinner with your neighbors.*

- *Serve finger foods at your home after church the Sunday before Christmas.*

There is no name so sweet on earth,

no name so sweet in heaven,

The name, before His wondrous birth,

to Christ the Savior given.

GEORGE W. BETHUNE

HE IS THE IMAGE OF THE INVISIBLE GOD, THE
FIRSTBORN OVER ALL CREATION.

COLOSSIANS 1:15

THIS IS HOW THE BIRTH OF JESUS CHRIST CAME ABOUT: HIS MOTHER MARY WAS PLEDGED TO BE MARRIED TO JOSEPH, BUT BEFORE THEY CAME TOGETHER, SHE WAS FOUND TO BE WITH CHILD THROUGH THE HOLY SPIRIT.

MATTHEW 1:18

AWAY IN A MANGER

Away in a manger, no crib for a bed,
The little Lord Jesus laid down His sweet head;
The stars in the bright sky looked down where He lay,
The Little Lord Jesus asleep on the hay.

The cattle are lowing, the Baby awakes,
But little Lord Jesus, no crying He makes;
I love thee, Lord Jesus! Look down from the sky,
And stay by my cradle till morning is nigh.

MARTIN LUTHER

THE GIFT

What can I give Him,
Poor as I am?
If I were a shepherd
I would bring a lamb.
If I were a Wise Man
I would do my part.
Yet what can I give Him?
I give Him my heart.

CHRISTINA ROSSETTI

MAKING CHRISTMAS FUN AND MEMORABLE FOR A SHUT-IN

- *Spend time in conversation together. Ask about Christmases gone by. Let your friend do the talking.*

- *Take a miniature decorated Christmas tree to brighten the home.*

- *Offer to help your friend with shopping, wrapping, and delivering gifts.*

- *Offer to make your friend's favorite Christmas cookies.*

- *Invite your friend to your home for a Christmas brunch or dinner. If homebound, take your friend a warm Christmas dinner on a bright holiday plate with a small poinsettia to brighten the day.*

SPECIAL THINGS TO DO
ON CHRISTMAS EVE

- *Enjoy homemade soup and sandwiches.*

- *Allow each family member to open one gift.*

- *Give everyone a new pair of pajamas.*

- *Make memories with photographs.*

- *Discuss the Nativity and the events surrounding the birth of Christ.*

- *Read the Christmas Story from the Bible.*

- *Sing Christmas carols together.*

- *Form a circle and allow each member of the family to offer a Christmas prayer.*

- *Offer thanksgiving for special times during the past year.*

Christ was one child Who knew more than His parents —

yet He obeyed them.

AND THE CHILD GREW AND BECAME STRONG; HE
WAS FILLED WITH WISDOM, AND THE GRACE OF
GOD WAS UPON HIM.

LUKE 2:40

A Christian is one who makes it easier

for other people to believe in God.

Sing hey!
Sing hey!
For Christmas Day;
Twin mistletoe
And holly,
For friendship
Glows
In winter snows,
And so let's all
Be jolly.

THE PERFECT GIFTS FOR SHUT-INS

- *Stamped envelopes*
- *Box of stationery or greeting cards*
- *Pens and pencils*
- *Brush and comb sets*
- *White socks*
- *A robe*
- *Toiletries and bath products*

CHRISTMAS WITH THE ROOSEVELTS

Although at least half of the Roosevelts' twelve years in the White House (1933 to 1945) were marked by war, First Lady Eleanor Roosevelt always made sure Christmas was a festive, family occasion. Each January, she would begin to fill a closet with Christmas presents for family and hundreds of friends, keeping a detailed log of her purchases.

Then every year on Christmas Eve, sitting near the Christmas tree and fireplace, President Franklin D. Roosevelt would read and recite from memory the Charles Dickens classic, A Christmas Carol.

It is good to be children sometimes,

and never better than at Christmas.

CHARLES DICKENS

A CHRISTMAS BLESSING
December 24, 1943

On behalf of the American people—your own people—I send this Christmas message to you, to you who are in our armed forces:

We ask God's blessing upon you—upon your fathers, (and) mothers, and wives and children— all your loved ones at home. We ask that the comfort of God's grace shall be granted to those who are sick and wounded, and to those who are prisoners of war in the hands of the enemy, waiting for the day when they will again be free.

And we ask that God receive and cherish those who have given their lives, and that He keep them in honor and in the grateful memory of their countrymen forever.

God bless all of you who fight our battles on this Christmas Eve.

God bless us all. [God] keep us strong in our faith that we fight for a better day for human-kind—here and everywhere.

PRESIDENT FRANKLIN DELANO ROOSEVELT
FIRESIDE CHAT
BROADCAST FROM HYDE PARK, N.Y.

Keeping Christmas is good,

but sharing it with others

is even better.

Let all your words be kind, and you will

always hear kind echoes.

BE KIND AND COMPASSIONATE TO ONE
ANOTHER, FORGIVING EACH OTHER, JUST AS IN
CHRIST GOD FORGAVE YOU.

EPHESIANS 4:32

And I do come home at Christmas. We all do, or we all should. We all come home, or ought to come home, for a short holiday — the longer, the better — from the great boarding school, where we are forever working at our arithmetical slates, to take, and give a rest.

CHARLES DICKENS

DID YOU KNOW?

Christmas trees still were considered a quaint foreign custom until 1850, when they were finally becoming quite fashionable in the eastern part of the United States.

How beautiful to walk in the steps of the Savior,

led in paths of light.

E. HEWITT

THOUGH I SIT IN DARKNESS, THE LORD
WILL BE MY LIGHT.

MICAH 7:8

The best way to cheer yourself up is

to try to cheer somebody else up.

MARK TWAIN

GIFTS A NEW FATHER WOULD LOVE

- *A picture frame suitable for his desk at work*

- *A romantic candlelight dinner spent with his wife*

- *A relaxing tape or CD*

- *A gift certificate for his favorite golf course*

- *A magazine subscription*

- *A tin filled with pretzels to enjoy as he watches the bowl games*

GIFTS A NEW MOTHER WOULD LOVE

- *Bath oil beads*
- *A gift certificate to her favorite restaurant*
- *A year's membership at the local spa*
- *Chocolate treats*
- *A book of short stories*
- *A mom's brag book*

HISTORY OF THE CANDY CANE

In the late 1800s, a candy maker in Indiana wanted to express the meaning of Christmas through a symbol made of candy. He came up with the idea of bending one of his white candy sticks into the shape of a cane and incorporating several symbols of Christ's love and sacrifice. First, he used a plain white peppermint stick. The color white symbolizes the purity and sinless nature of Jesus.

Next, he added three small stripes to symbolize the pain inflicted upon Jesus before His death on the cross. He added a bold stripe to represent the blood Jesus shed for mankind. When looked at with the crook on top, it looks like a shepherd's staff, because Jesus is the Shepherd of man. If you turn it upside down, it becomes the letter "J," symbolizing the first letter in Jesus' name. The candy cane serves as a lasting reminder of what Christmas is really all about.

WISE MEN STILL SEEK HIM

AFTER JESUS WAS BORN IN BETHLEHEM IN JUDEA,
DURING THE TIME OF KING HEROD, MAGI
FROM THE EAST CAME TO JERUSALEM AND
ASKED, "WHERE IS THE ONE WHO HAS BEEN
BORN KING OF THE JEWS?" ON COMING TO THE
HOUSE, THEY SAW THE CHILD WITH HIS
MOTHER MARY, AND THEY BOWED DOWN AND
WORSHIPED HIM. THEN THEY OPENED THEIR
TREASURES AND PRESENTED HIM WITH GIFTS OF
GOLD AND OF INCENSE AND MYRRH.

MATTHEW 2:1,2,11

80

WE THREE KINGS OF ORIENT ARE

We three kings of Orient are,
bearing gifts we traverse afar,
field and fountain, moor and mountain,
following yonder star.

O, star of wonder, star of night,
star with royal beauty bright,
westward leading, still proceeding,
guide us to Thy perfect light.

ENJOY A LIGHT BREAKFAST ON CHRISTMAS MORNING

- *Freshly baked muffins*
- *Holiday pound cake*
- *Freshly squeezed orange juice*
- *Hot chocolate*
- *Coffee*

HOLIDAY POUND CAKE

1 pound butter
1 pound light brown sugar
6 eggs
1 1/2 teaspoons vanilla
4 cups plain flour

1/2 teaspoon salt
2 cups pecans, chopped
1/2 pound candied cherries
1/2 pound candied pineapple

Cream butter and sugar together. Add eggs, one at a time, beating well after each. Add flavoring. Slowly add dry ingredients. Stir in nuts and fruit. Bake at 325 degrees for one hour or until done.

SPECIAL GIFTS FOR ANIMALS

- *Make a charitable donation to your local animal shelter.*

- *Adopt a pet that needs a home.*

- *Spread peanut butter on a pine cone and roll it in birdseed. Hang it from a tree in your yard.*

- *Tie red ribbons in your dog's hair.*

84

- *Put a festive collar on your cat.*

- *Buy a new plastic feeding bowl and paint holly and berries around the outside of it.*

- *Make your dog his own special Christmas tree. Adorn it with dog biscuits, tied on with red ribbon. Place a small stuffed animal on top.*

And every beast, by some good spell,

In the stable dark was glad to tell,

Of the gift he gave Immanuel,

The gift he gave Immanuel.

Take time to laugh in this season of joy.

It is the music of the soul!

PRESIDENTIAL CHRISTMAS CARDS

Before 1953, most presidential greeting cards were unofficial. Then President Dwight Eisenhower and his wife, Mamie, conferred with their good friend, Joyce Hall, the founder of Hallmark Cards. The result was an official presidential Christmas card, embossed with the presidential seal, and sent to ambassadors, heads of state, high-ranking government officials, White House staffers, and friends.

That first year, only 1,110 cards were prepared. In 1998, the White House expected to send out at least 300,000.

The President and Mrs. Eisenhower extend their

best wishes for Christmas and the New Year.

(Inscription on the first official
White House Christmas card)

SNOW-CAPPED CHOCOLATE COOKIES

$1/2$ cup vegetable shortening
$1^2/3$ cups sugar
2 teaspoons vanilla extract
2 eggs
2 1-ounce squares unsweetened chocolate, melted
2 cups sifted all-purpose flour
$1/2$ teaspoon salt
2 teaspoons baking powder
$1/3$ cup milk
$1/2$ cup chopped walnuts
Confectioners' sugar

In a large bowl, cream shortening, sugar, and vanilla, with mixer on medium, until light. Beat in eggs. Stir in chocolate until well blended. Sift together dry ingredients. Blend into creamed mixture, alternately with milk. Stir in nuts. Chill for three hours. Form dough into 1-inch balls. Roll in confectioners' sugar. Place 2 to 3 inches apart on greased cookie sheet. Bake for 15 minutes. Cool slightly. Remove from pan. Dust with additional confectioners' sugar.

Makes about 48 cookies.

JOIN ALL THE GLORIOUS NAMES

Join all the glorious names of wisdom,
love and pow'r,
that ever mortals knew,
that angels ever bore:
All are too poor to speak His worth,
too poor to set my Savior forth.
Great Prophet of my God,
my tongue would bless Thy name;
By Thee the joyful news
of our salvation came:
The joyful news of sins forgiv'n,
of hell subdued, and peace with heav'n.

THE MOST IMPORTANT THINGS YOU CAN GIVE ON CHRISTMAS

- *Your time—Volunteer to help those less fortunate.*

- *Your love—It's the thought that counts.*

- *Your life—Jesus was born that you might be saved.*

- *Your Lord—Share Jesus with your friends and family.*

My Savior and my Lord,
*   my Conq'ror and my King,*
Thy scepter and Thy sword,
*   Thy reigning grace I sing:*
Thine is the pow'r—behold I sit
*   in willing bonds beneath Thy feet.*

Now let my soul arise
   and tread the tempter down;
My Captain leads me forth
   to conquest and a crown:
A feeble saint shall win the day,
   tho death and hell obstruct the way.

CHRISTMAS SUGAR SNOWDROPS!

1 cup sugar
2 sticks (1 cup) butter or margarine, softened to
*   room temperature*
1/2 teaspoon almond extract
1/2 teaspoon vanilla extract
1 egg, lightly beaten
2 cups all-purpose flour
1/2 cup finely chopped pecans or walnuts
Sugar

Cream sugar and butter in mixing bowl. Add extracts and egg; beat until fluffy. Beat in flour and nuts until mixture is lightly moistened. Chill for 1 hour or until dough is easily handled. Preheat oven to 350°. Shape dough into 1-inch balls. Place on greased cookie sheet, 2 inches apart. Using a flat-bottomed glass, dip glass into sugar, then press balls to a 1/4-inch thickness. Sprinkle with more sugar, if desired. Bake for 10 to 12 minutes or until cookies are lightly golden.

Makes 3 dozen.

HISTORY OF THE CHRISTMAS TREE

The Christmas tree originated in Germany in the sixteenth century. It was common for the German people to decorate fir trees, both inside and out, with roses, apples, and colored paper.

It is believed that Martin Luther, the Protestant reformer, was the first to light a Christmas tree with candles. While coming home one dark winter's night near Christmas, Luther was struck with the beauty of the starlight shining through the branches of a small fir tree outside his home. He duplicated the starlight by using candles attached to the branches of his indoor Christmas tree.

The three wise men saw the light and followed it.

They are rightly called wise!

O LORD, OUR LORD, HOW MAJESTIC IS YOUR
NAME IN ALL THE EARTH!

PSALM 8:9

If . . . we open our hearts and embrace Him . . .

not only to reap abundance and joy and health

and happy fulfillment, but also for

the cancellation of our sins — then this is the

greatest welcome we can give to the Christ Child.

NORMAN VINCENT PEALE

MARY TREASURED UP ALL THESE THINGS
AND PONDERED THEM IN HER HEART.

LUKE 2:19

101

JOY TO THE WORLD

Joy to the world! The Lord is come!
  Let earth receive her King;
Let ev'ry heart prepare Him room,
  And heav'n and nature sing.
Joy to the earth, the Savior reigns.
  Let men their songs employ,
While fields and floods, rocks, hills, and plains
  Repeat the sounding joy.

No more let sins and sorrows grow,
*   Nor thorns infest the ground;*
He comes to make His blessings flow
*   Far as the curse is found.*
He rules the world with truth and grace,
*   And makes the nations prove*
The glories of His righteousness
*   And wonders of His love.*

BUT WHEN THE TIME HAD FULLY COME,
GOD SENT HIS SON, BORN OF A WOMAN,
BORN UNDER LAW, TO REDEEM THOSE
UNDER LAW, THAT WE MIGHT RECEIVE THE
FULL RIGHTS OF SONS.

GALATIANS 4:4

Christmas, my child, is love in action.

Every time we love, every time we give,

it's Christmas.

DALE EVANS

I will honor Christmas in my heart and try

to keep it all the year.

CHARLES DICKENS

DID YOU KNOW?

- *In 1836, Alabama was the first state in the U.S. to declare Christmas a legal holiday.*

- *In 1907, Oklahoma became the last U.S. state to declare Christmas a legal holiday.*

CHRISTMAS IN GREECE

Christmas is one of the most holy, religious holidays celebrated throughout Greece. During this time, it is customary to bake traditional Christmas cakes, or kouloures, which are decorated with a symbol of the family's profession. Farmers draw a plough or grapes; shepherds' wives scribe a stable, sheep, or a shepherd on the dough. Then a coin is baked into one of the cakes.

In days of old, before the bread was eaten, it would be blessed by the village vicar, and the coin would be given to the priest for the church. The ceremony of passing out the bread was much like the celebration of Communion.

Today, the oldest member of the family makes the sign of the cross on the bread with his knife, and then parts are broken off—the first for Jesus, another for Mary, and then one for each family member. It is believed the person who receives the coin will live a blessed year.

Do give books —religious or otherwise —for Christmas.

They're never fattening, seldom sinful,

and permanently personal.

LENORA HERSHEY

EVERY GOOD AND PERFECT GIFT IS FROM ABOVE,
COMING DOWN FROM THE FATHER.

JAMES 1:17

DID YOU KNOW?

- *Until the 1860s, Christmas was not a big celebration in America, primarily because of our Puritan heritage. Boston Puritans had banned the celebration of Christmas.*

- *The Christmas tree has not always been a part of our holiday celebration in America. It was first introduced to the United States during the American Revolution by Hessian troops, and the tradition continued with German settlers in eastern Pennsylvania.*

CHRISTMAS GIFT IDEAS
FOR LESS THAN $5.00

- *A Christmas ornament*
- *A pre-paid phone card*
- *Note Cards*
- *Something for a pet*
- *Christmas socks*
- *A small book*

GOD ALWAYS REMEMBERS YOU

There was a lady in the state hospital. She carried the card a friend of ours sent her in a little drawstring bag, and during the entire Christmas season, she would stop people and say, "Look at my Christmas card. The lady I worked for sent it to me. I'm not forgotten." We heard later that card, the only one she received, was the beginning of her recovery.

REAMER KLINE

VOICES IN THE MIST

The time draws near the birth of Christ:

The moon is hid; the night is still;

The Christmas bells from hill to hill

Answer each other in the mist.

Four voices of four hamlets round,

From far and near, on mead and moor,

Swell out and fail, as if a door

Were shut between me and the sound:

Each voice four changes on the wind,

That now dilate, and now decrease,

Peace and goodwill, goodwill and peace,

Peace and goodwill, to all mankind.

ALFRED, LORD TENNYSON

PEANUT BRITTLE

¹/₂ cup water
2 cups sugar
1 cup corn syrup
2 Tbsp. butter
2 cups whole blanched peanuts
1 tsp. baking soda

Butter (or cover with parchment paper) two cookie sheets. In a heavy pot, on medium heat, combine water, sugar, and corn syrup. Bring to boil, stirring continuously.

Continue boiling until a candy thermometer reads 300 degrees or until syrup reaches the hard-crack stage when you drip a drop of it into cold water. Remove from the heat, and stir in the butter, peanuts and baking soda. Use caution, because the baking soda will cause the mixture to foam.
Pour the brittle onto the cookie sheets and quickly spread with a hot spatula. When it has hardened, break into pieces.

(Makes about 2 pounds of peanut brittle.)

NO GLASS BETWEEN

The story is told of a little boy whose family was quite poor. Since he never received any gifts at Christmastime, he would stand and press his nose against the store windows, staring at all the clothes and toys other little boys would find under their trees.

One day, the little boy dashed out in front of a car to save a kitten and was struck. Passersby called for help, and he was rushed to a nearby hospital.

Because it was Christmas, one of the nurses bought him a troop of toy soldiers and laid them in his lap. His eyes were wide as he gently touched them. "What do you think?" the nurse asked.

"There isn't any glass between!"

Someday, we shall see Christ face to face, with no "glass" in-between.

GIFTS FOR THE PERSON WHO HAS EVERYTHING

- *Memory Box —Fill a fancy box with memories from when you and that person were younger.*

- *Movie Rental —Give them movie-rental certificates in a basket with a bag of microwave popcorn and soda.*

- *Mall Gift Certificate —Decide how much you want to spend and purchase a gift certificate at the mall office.*

- *Thoughtful Basket — Buy a basket and fill it with all their favorite things — candy, bath oil, and scented candles.*

- *Dinner — Fix up a basket with everything they need for a nice dinner at home, including entrée, salad, and dessert.*

DID YOU KNOW?

Saint Nicholas was a fourth century bishop of Myra, located in what is now called Turkey. He was the patron saint of children, as well as sailors, because he would secretly deliver money or presents to the poor and also was credited with calming the raging sea.

PEACE ON EARTH AMONG MEN OF GOODWILL!

This is the blessed promise of Christmas. It is the perfect antidote for any fear or hysteria that may enter our lives.

WHILE BY OUR SHEEP

While by our sheep we watched at night,
glad tidings bro't an angel bright.
There shall be born, so he did say,
in Bethlehem a Child today.
There shall the Child lie in a stall,
this Child who shall redeem us all,
This gift of God we'll cherish well
—Jesus, our Lord Emanuel.

A joy that is shared is a joy made double.

JOHN ROY

ARE YOU READY FOR CHRISTMAS?

Are you willing to stoop down and consider the needs and desires of little children; to remember the weaknesses and loneliness of people who are growing old; to stop asking how much your friends love you, and to ask yourself whether you love them enough; to bear in mind the things that other people have to bear on their hearts;

. . . to trim your lamp so that it will give more light and less smoke, and to carry it in front so that your shadow will fall behind you; to make a grave for your ugly thoughts and a garden for your kindly feelings, with the gate open? Are you willing to do these things for a day? Then you are ready for Christmas!

HENRY VAN DYKE

Let's approach Christmas with an expectant hush, rather than a last-minute rush.

A CHRISTMAS BLESSING

God grant you the light in Christmas, which is faith; the warmth of Christmas, which is love; the radiance of Christmas, which is purity; the righteousness of Christmas, which is justice; the belief in Christmas, which is truth; the all of Christmas, which is Christ.

WILDA ENGLISH

129

SENTIMENTAL GIFTS FOR LOVED ONES:

- *Homemade ornaments created out of old lace or heirloom tablecloths*

- *A favorite family recipe passed down through the generations*

- *A piece of art made from your children's handprints and finger paint*

- *Cuttings from your favorite greenhouse plants, potted and wrapped with a holiday bow*

It is not the gift, but the thought that counts.

VAN DYKE

It is Christmas in the mansion,
Yule-log fires and silken frocks;
It is Christmas in the cottage,
Mother's filling little socks.

It is Christmas on the highway,
In the thronging, busy mart;
But the dearest, truest Christmas
Is the Christmas in the heart.

So remember while December
Brings the only Christmas Day,
In the year let there be Christmas
In the things you do and say;

Wouldn't life be worth the living
Wouldn't dreams be coming true
If we kept the Christmas spirit
All the whole year through?

IT HAPPENED ON CHRISTMAS DAY

In 1939, Montgomery Ward stores introduced Rudolph as the ninth reindeer. The stores gave away more than 2.4 million copies of a little booklet called "Rudolf the Red-Nose Reindeer." The poem was written by Robert May, who worked in the advertising department, and illustrated by Denver Gillen.

Famous cowboy singer, Gene Autry, immortalized Rudolf in his 1949 hit record, and people continue to sing it every Christmas.

Remembrance, like a candle,

burns brightest at Christmastime.

CHARLES DICKENS

THE TRUE LIGHT THAT GIVES LIGHT TO EVERY
MAN WAS COMING INTO THE WORLD.

JOHN 1:9

DID YOU KNOW?

The word Christmas, or "Christ's Mass," comes from the Latin: Cristes maesse. Most historians believe Christmas was first celebrated in 336 ad in Rome.

MOST POPULAR CHRISTMAS TREE VARIETIES

- *Scotch pine*
- *Douglas fir*
- *Noble fir*
- *Fraser fir*
- *Virginia pine*
- *Balsam fir*
- *White pine*

Merry Christmas

Born in a stable, Cradled in a manger, In the world His hands had made, Born a stranger.

CHRISTINE GEORGINA ROSSETTI

FOR GOD SO LOVED THE WORLD THAT HE GAVE HIS ONE AND ONLY SON, THAT WHOEVER BELIEVES IN HIM SHALL NOT PERISH BUT HAVE ETERNAL LIFE.

JOHN 3:16

Christianity is not a religion, it is a relationship.

DR. THIEME

THE VIRGIN WILL BE WITH CHILD AND
WILL GIVE BIRTH TO A SON, AND THEY WILL CALL
HIM IMMANUEL—WHICH MEANS,
"GOD WITH US."

MATTHEW 1:23

CHRISTMAS IN BRAZIL

Father Christmas is called Papai Noël in Brazil, where Christmas is a summer holiday. For many Brazilians, the Christmas meal will consist of pork, chicken, turkey, ham, rice, salad, and fresh and dried fruits. The less fortunate will eat chicken and rice to celebrate the birth of the Christ Child.

THE ORIGIN OF CHRISTMAS PUDDING

Because of their British roots, more than forty million people finish off their holiday meal with Christmas pudding. The dessert originated in the fourteenth century as a porridge called frumenty. It was made by boiling beef and mutton with currants, prunes, raisins, wine, and spices. By 1595, frumenty was evolving into plum pudding by adding eggs, bread crumbs, dried fruit, and ale.

Christmas living is the best kind of

Christmas giving.

VAN DYKE

DID YOU KNOW?

In 1805, Thomas Jefferson celebrated Christmas with one hundred guests, including his six grandchildren, by playing a merry jig on his fiddle.

The way you spend Christmas is far more important than how much.

HENRY DAVID THOREAU

CHRISTMAS WITH PRESIDENT ANDREW JACKSON

It is reported that President Jackson loved to spend Christmas having a snowball fight with children from a local orphanage. His wife had died early in their marriage, and he shared his home with relatives. Because his own mother had died when he was a boy, he had never received any toys for Christmas. So he made sure there were plenty of gifts under the tree for everyone.

WHEN CHRISTMAS IS OVER

We've put away the ornaments,
And burned the Christmas tree;
The Christmas fun is over — but
The Christ Child, where is He?

He lives in gifts and toys we share
With children who have few
And in the acts of kindness
We do the whole year through.

CORINNA MARSH

I never realized God's birth before,

How He grew likest God in being born . . .

Such ever love's way — to rise, it stoops.

ROBERT BROWNING

Christmas began in the heart of God.

It is complete only when it reaches

the heart of man.

Were earth a thousand times as fair,

Beset with gold and jewels rare,

She yet were far too poor to be

A narrow cradle, Lord, for Thee.

MARTIN LUTHER

I saw a stable, low and very bare,

A little child in a manger.

The oxen knew Him, had Him in their care,

To men He was a stranger.

The safety of the world was lying there,

And the world's danger.

MARY ELIZABETH COLERIDGE

While shepherds watched

their flocks by night,

All seated on the ground,

The angel of the Lord came down,

And glory shone around.

NAHUM TATE

IDEAS FOR CHRISTMAS DINNER LEFTOVERS

- *Use stuffing to season your favorite meat loaf recipe.*

- *Dice mushroom stems and mix with stuffing, then fill caps and bake until hot.*

- *Add cream cheese, sour cream, and chives to mashed potatoes and reheat.*

- *Add cubed ham to beaten eggs; scramble and top with shredded cheddar cheese.*

- *Mix diced ham with drained crushed pineapple, shredded carrots, walnuts, and mayonnaise.*

- *Mix cubed ham into macaroni and cheese.*

- *Toss romaine lettuce with croutons, Parmesan cheese, and Caesar dressing, then lay strips of turkey on top.*

Here is love, that

God sent His Son,

His Son who never offended,

His Son who was always

His delight.

JOHN BUNYAN

IMMENSE IN MERCY AND WITH AN
INCREDIBLE LOVE, [GOD] EMBRACED US.
HE TOOK OUR SIN-DEAD LIVES
AND MADE US ALIVE IN CHRIST.

EPHESIANS 2:4,5 THE MESSAGE

The way to Christmas lies through an
ancient gate. . . . It is a little gate, child-high,
child-wide, and there is a password:
"Peace on earth to men of good will."
May you, this Christmas, become as a little child
again and enter into His kingdom.

ANGELO PATRI

Those who know Christ

know the source of Joy.

CHARLES R. HEMBREE

JESUS CHRIST IS THE SAME YESTERDAY,
TODAY, AND FOREVER.

HEBREWS 13:8 TLB

Additional copies of this book and other Christmas titles
are available from your local bookstore.

A Treasury of Christmas Joy
The Wonder of Christmas
God's Little Christmas Book
Everything I Need to Know About Christmas I Learned from Jesus
Christmas Treasures of the Heart
The Greatest Christmas Ever
The Christmas Cookie Cookbook
The Candymaker's Gift
The Living Nativity
The Indescribable Gift

If you have enjoyed this book, or if it has
impacted your life, we would like to hear from you.

Please contact us at:
Honor Books
Department E
P.O. Box 55388
Tulsa, Oklahoma 74155
Or by e-mail at info@honorbooks.com